152.1423 Mayerlin
Patterns in spring

TOOLS FOR TEACHERS

- **ATOS:** 0.8
- **LEXILE:** 50L
- **CURRICULUM CONNECTIONS:** patterns, sorting
- **WORD COUNT:** 57

Skills to Teach

- **HIGH-FREQUENCY WORDS:** a, at, has, is, look, the, what
- **CONTENT WORDS:** boots, eggs, flowers, grass, kite, pattern, umbrella
- **PUNCTUATION:** periods, question marks, exclamation point
- **WORD STUDY:** dipthong /ou/, spelled ow (*flowers*); double consonants (*eggs, grass, pattern, umbrella*); oo, pronounced as short /oo/ (*look*), long /oo/ (*boots*)
- **TEXT TYPE:** factual description

Before Reading Activities

- Read the title and give a simple statement of the main idea.
- Have students "walk" though the book and talk about what they see in the pictures.
- Introduce new vocabulary by having students predict the first letter and locate the word in the text.
- Discuss any unfamiliar concepts that are in the text.

After Reading Activities

Write the book's language pattern in two columns on the board: "Look at the ____." and "What is the pattern?" Encourage children to look around the room and identify things that have patterns. Write their answers under the first column. Then identify and discuss the different kinds of patterns they see (stripes, spots, etc.), and write them down under the second column.

Tadpole Books are published by Jump!, 5357 Penn Avenue South, Minneapolis, MN 55419, www.jumplibrary.com

Copyright ©2018 Jump. International copyright reserved in all countries. No part of this book may be reproduced in any form without written permission from the publisher.

Editor: Jenny Fretland VanVoorst **Designer:** Anna Peterson

Photo Credits: Dreamstime: Olesia Bilkei, 10–11. iStock: mediaphotos, 2–3. Shutterstock: topnatthapon, cover; Andrej Antic, 1; Sergey Tinyakov, 4–5; Sergey Novikov, 6–7; Scisetti Alfio, 8–9; skywing, 8–9; Rafal Olkis, 12–13; Cathy Keifer, 14–15.

Library of Congress Cataloging-in-Publication Data is available at www.loc.gov or upon request from the publisher.
Names: Mayerling, Tim, author.
Title: Patterns in spring / by Tim Mayerling.
Description: Minneapolis, Minnesota: Jump!, Inc., 2017. | Series: Patterns in the seasons | Audience: Ages 3–6. | Includes index.
Identifiers: LCCN 2017018073 (print) | LCCN 2017022665 (ebook) | ISBN 9781624966040 (ebook) | ISBN 9781620317570 (hardcover: alk. paper) | ISBN 9781620317778 (pbk.)
Subjects: LCSH: Pattern perception—Juvenile literature. | Spring—Juvenile literature.
Classification: LCC BF294 (ebook) | LCC BF294 .M385 2017 (print) | DDC 152.14/23—dc23
LC record available at https://lccn.loc.gov/2017018073

PATTERNS IN SPRING

by Tim Mayerling

TABLE OF CONTENTS

tadpole
books

PATTERNS IN SPRING

Look at the boots.

What is the pattern?

egg

Look at the eggs.

What is the pattern?

kite

Look at the kite.

What is the pattern?

Look at the flowers.

What is the pattern?

Look at the umbrella.

What is the pattern?

Look at the grass.

What is the pattern?

Look!

What else has a pattern?

WORDS TO KNOW

boots

eggs

flowers

grass

kite

umbrella

INDEX